HENRY FORD

—Putting the WORLD on WHEELS—

By the Editors of TIME FOR KIDS
WITH DINA EL NABLI

Collins
An Imprint of HarperCollins*Publishers*

About the Author: Dina El Nabli is a writer, editor, and website producer. The author lives in New Jersey with her family.

Library of Congress Cataloging-in-Publication Data is available.
ISBN 978-0-06-057630-1 (pbk). — ISBN 978-0-06-057631-8 (trade)

13 14 15 16 17 SCP 10 9
First Edition

Copyright © by Time Inc.

TIME For Kids and the Red Border Design are Trademarks of Time Inc. used under license.

Photography and Illustration Credits:
Cover: ©AP/Wide World photos; cover inset: ©Pixtal/SuperStock; cover flap: ©National Motor Museum/Topham—HIP/The Image Works; title page: The Henry Ford; contents page: The Henry Ford; p.iv: Public Domain; p.1: (all chapter titles): Ford Motor Company; p.1 (bottom): ©Mary Evans Picture Collection; p.2 (top): From the Collections of The Henry Ford; pp.2-3 (bottom): From the Collections of The Henry Ford; p.4: From the Collections of The Henry Ford; p.5: From the Collections of The Henry Ford; p.6 (top): From the Collections of The Henry Ford; p.6 (bottom): From the Collections of The Henry Ford; p.7: ©AP/Wide World Photos; p.8: Underwood & Underwood/CORBIS; p.9: Library of Congress; p.10: From the Collections of The Henry Ford; p.11: From the Collections of The Henry Ford; p.12: From the Collections of The Henry Ford; p.13 (top): From the Collections of The Henry Ford; p. 13 (bottom): From the Collections of The Henry Ford; p.14: From the Collections of The Henry Ford; p.15: From the Collections of The Henry Ford; p.16: From the Collections of The Henry Ford; p.17: From the Collections of The Henry Ford; p.18: From the Collections of The Henry Ford; p.19: ©The Granger Collection, NY; p.20: From the Collections of The Henry Ford; p.21: From the Collections of The Henry Ford; p.22: ©The Granger Collection, NY: p.23: ©Thinkstock/Punchstock; p.24: ©Mary Evans Picture Collection; p.25: ©Bettmann/CORBIS; p.26: From the Collections of The Henry Ford; p.27: From the Collections of The Henry Ford; p.28: ©Swim Ink2, LLC/CORBIS; p.29: From the Collections of The Henry Ford; p.30: From the Collections of The Henry Ford; p.31: From the Collections of The Henry Ford; p.32: The Granger Collection, NY; p.33: From the Collections of The Henry Ford; p.34: ©Herbert Gehr/Time Life Pictures/Getty Images; p.35: ©Wolfgang Kaehler/CORBIS; p.36: From the Collections of The Henry Ford; p.37: From the Collections of The Henry Ford; p.38: U.S. Naval Photography Center; p.39 (top): ©Robert Holmes/CORBIS; p. 39 (bottom): From the Collections of The Henry Ford; p.40: ©AP/Wide World Photos; p.41: ©Ralph Morse/Time Life Pictures/Getty Images; p.42: Courtesy The Henry Ford; p.43 (top): Courtesy The Henry Ford; p.43 (bottom): Courtesy The Henry Ford; p.44 (from top): Underwood & Underwood/CORBIS; Library of Congress; ©Photographer's Choice by Getty Images/Punchstock; ©Mary Evans Picture Library/Everett Collection; back cover: Handout/Getty Images

Acknowledgments:
For TIME FOR KIDS: Designer: Colleen Pidel; Photography Editor: Jacqui Wong

 Find out more at www.timeforkids.com/bio/ford

CONTENTS

"*Enthusiasm is the yeast that makes your hopes shine to the stars.*"

—HENRY FORD

◄ This is the first photo of Henry Ford when he began the Ford Motor Company in 1904.

CHAPTER 1

THE NEW
FAMILY
CAR

The year was 1906. In a secret room on the third floor of a factory in Detroit, Michigan, a group of workers gathered around a chalkboard. Henry Ford, their leader, had a big idea: He wanted to create a new kind of car.

In those days cars were very hard to build. They were heavy and expensive, and few people owned them. Ford wanted to change that. In 1906 Henry wrote a letter to a magazine explaining his idea. "The greatest need today is a light, low-priced car with an up-to-date engine of ample horsepower, and built of the very best material," he

▲ AN EARLY AD said, "All the world loves a Ford. Even the moon beams."

1

wrote. He wanted to build a lightweight car that everyone could afford. In the secret room in Michigan, workers listened closely as Henry talked about this new kind of car. They drew models of the car on the chalkboard. Together they brought their ideas to life.

Henry sat in what was once his mother's rocking chair as he studied the plans on the board. He had brought the comfortable chair in for good luck. Hour by hour and day by day, new ideas were drawn out. Engineers and designers worked as a team.

Excitement began to build. Something special was happening.

One day Henry and his team made an important discovery. They found a new kind of steel that was lighter and cheaper than what was being used in other cars. The vanadium steel was used to build Ford's new model. The new car was not only lighter, but it was also big enough to seat five people. Ford's older cars were only big enough for two.

In 1908 the new car was finally ready for the public. Ford called it the Model T. Over the next nineteen years, Ford built more than 15 million Model Ts. By 1928 half the cars in the world were Model Ts! The car that was sketched out in the secret room of that Detroit factory forever changed America—and the world.

▼ FORD CARS take a spin in a snowy Detroit in 1906.

CHAPTER 2

LIFE ON THE
FARM

The man who put the world on wheels was born on a farm in what is today Dearborn, Michigan. Back then Dearborn was a rural area with wide-open spaces.

In 1847 Henry's father, William Ford, moved from Ireland to America. He hoped for a better life in eastern Michigan. William got a job as a worker on the family farm of a young girl named Mary Litogot O'Hern. Years later William and Mary married. They settled nearby on another farm.

Henry was born on July 30, 1863,

▲ **THIS EARLY** photo of Henry was taken about 1866.

▲ IN 1863 Henry Ford was born in this Michigan farmhouse.

in the Fords' home. He was the oldest of six children. Henry and his brothers and sisters—John, Margaret, Jane, William Jr., and Robert—went to a one-room school and also worked in the fields to help their family.

Henry never liked farming, but he loved experimenting with gadgets. He especially liked tinkering with watches. Sometimes he would take different watches apart just to see if he could put them back together again.

Henry was always curious. He dreamed of ways to make farming chores easier. Was there a better way to plow and haul on the farm? Henry was determined to find out.

After Henry turned seven, his father sent him to the Scotch Settlement School.

▲ MARY LITOGOT O'HERN encouraged her son to experiment.

He was excited to be going to the same school his mother, Mary, attended when she was a girl. At school Henry met Edsel Ruddiman. The boys played together and became best friends.

Mary Ford wanted to encourage Henry's curiosity. She asked William to build Henry his own workbench. Henry loved having a place to work with his gadgets. When he wasn't in school, on the playground, or helping on the farm, Henry could be found tinkering.

Just before Henry turned thirteen in 1876, tragedy struck the Ford family. Mary Ford died.

▲ WILLIAM FORD expected his son to help on the family farm.

She was just thirty-seven. Henry missed his mother terribly. "The house was like a watch without a mainspring," he later wrote about his mother's death.

A Machine on the Move

One summer afternoon in 1876, Henry took a trip to Detroit with his father. Henry loved visiting the city and all of its machine shops. During the buggy ride, Henry saw something amazing. A steam engine loudly chugged its way along the road toward Henry and his father. It was the first

▶ AS A TEEN Henry was fascinated by machines.

road machine Henry had ever seen that could travel on its own power without the help of horses or mules.

Henry was fascinated at how steam was used to power the machine. He wondered if steam could be used to pull other types of machines. That was the day Henry knew he didn't want to be a farmer. Instead, he wanted to build machines that moved on their own.

▼ STEAM ENGINES such as this one inspired Henry to figure out a way to build a machine that carried people.

▲ HENRY moved to the big city of Detroit in 1879.

Three years later, in 1879, Henry decided it was time to pursue his dream. He was sixteen years old when he left the family farm for Detroit, where he moved in with his aunt, Rebecca Flaherty.

Henry's father helped get him a job as an apprentice at the James Flower & Brothers Machine Shop. An apprentice is someone who works for another person in order to learn a trade. There Henry learned about machine parts like valves and steam whistles. At night he earned extra money by repairing watches and clocks.

CHAPTER 3

HENRY
THE ENGINEER

In 1882 Henry returned to Dearborn. He was almost twenty and his father wanted Henry to help with the harvest and run the farm.

Henry still didn't want to be a farmer. Instead, he took a job traveling around parts of Michigan fixing steam engines for a company called Westinghouse. When he had the time, Henry took night classes studying accounting, typing, mechanical drawing, and business.

▶ HENRY was twenty-three when this photo was taken.

Henry and Clara

▲ CLARA JANE BRYANT
supported her husband in all he tried.

One night, when Henry was twenty-one, he met a young woman at a dance. Her name was Clara Jane Bryant. Like Henry, Clara came from a family of successful farmers. Henry and Clara had many of the same interests, including a love of music and dancing.

Before long, Henry and Clara began spending more time together, going on picnics and buggy rides. Clara loved hearing about Henry's experiments. She had so much faith in his ideas that he called her the Believer.

On April 11, 1888, three years after they met, Clara and Henry were married. They moved into their own farmhouse on the Ford family's property. But Henry was thinking about trying to get a job at the Edison Illuminating Company in Detroit. He thought it was the perfect place to work since he wanted to learn more about electricity, which was a fairly new way of lighting homes and powering some machines.

In 1891 the Fords left their farmhouse for a small apartment in Detroit. Times were tough in the city. Many people couldn't find a job. But Henry's experience and determination helped him. He landed a job working as a mechanical engineer for the Edison Illuminating Company.

Henry's hard work and talent quickly earned him better positions and higher pay. That wasn't the only good news for Henry and Clara. On November 6, 1893, Clara and Henry's first and only child was born. They named him Edsel, after Edsel Ruddiman, Henry's best friend from school.

At work, Henry continued to rise up the ranks at the Edison plant. The Fords moved to a new home on

▼ WORKERS at the Edison Illuminating Company, where Henry worked

▲ **IT'S A BOY!** Clara and Edsel pose for the camera in 1893.

Bagley Avenue so Henry could be closer to work. Their new house was one of the first in the city to be wired for electricity. It had a shed in the backyard where Henry could work on experiments. He was trying to build a gasoline engine that would power a car.

Henry spent many nights tinkering in the shed. On Christmas Eve in

HENRY FORD
& THOMAS EDISON

In the summer of 1896, Henry was invited to go to a business meeting in New York City. It was there that he met his idol, the father of electricity, Thomas Edison. Edison became one of Henry Ford's close friends. Both men loved the outdoors and camping. They were joined by other famous men such as tire maker Harvey Firestone.

After Edison moved to Fort Myers, Florida, Ford bought the vacation home next door. Today the Edison and Ford Winter Estates are open to the public.

In October 1929, on the 50th anniversary of the lightbulb, Henry honored Edison by establishing the Edison Institute at Greenfield Village. President Hoover and many famous Americans attended the celebration.

▼ HENRY FORD AND THOMAS EDISON

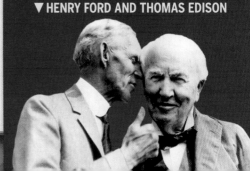

▲ HENRY built this model of a steam engine in 1893.
A lightbulb could run on the engine's power.

1893, he was ready to show Clara the experiment he had been working on. He had built a gas engine small enough to fit on the kitchen table. He needed Clara's help to get it started. Clara poured in the fuel while Henry spun the engine's flywheel. The engine came to life, filling the kitchen with thick, black smoke. The kitchen was a mess, but Henry's experiment was a success.

The Quadricycle

Early on the morning of June 4, 1896, Henry was ready to try out his latest invention. Henry called his new gas-powered vehicle a Quadricycle because it ran on four big bicycle tires. The car steered with a tiller just like a boat. It had two forward speeds but could not go in reverse. There was only one problem. The car couldn't fit through the door of the workshed! Henry took an ax and knocked a hole through the wall. Now he could get his car out of the shed.

Henry drove the Quadricycle through Detroit. The successful test drive made Henry more determined than ever to continue his work on gas engines.

Over the next several months people often saw Henry driving around town. He could cause quite a commotion because the noisy Quadricycle scared horses and drew crowds of curious people. Later Henry wrote: ". . . I had to get a special permit from the mayor and thus for a time enjoyed the distinction of being the only licensed chauffeur [driver] in America." Henry was thrilled with his success.

◀ THE QUADRICYCLE was the first vehicle Henry built.

CHAPTER 4

THE
BEGINNING

In 1898 Henry completed an improved version of his gas-powered vehicle. By the summer of 1899, he produced a third version. The car looked much more polished than Henry's Quadricycle. A Detroit newspaper wrote about Henry's latest invention. He was beginning to get noticed.

Detroit Mayor William Maybury believed in Henry's work. He decided to invest money to help Henry set up a company to build and sell cars. The Detroit Automobile Company was formed on August 5, 1899.

◄ HENRY in 1895

Henry's job was to design a line of cars and to make money selling them.

The company's first design was a delivery truck. It wasn't the lightweight, smooth-running car Henry had always wanted to build. In fact, it didn't run well at all. Henry wasn't able to turn the truck into a vehicle the public would buy. The new company was losing money. After less then two years, the Detroit Automobile Company went out of business.

Though the Detroit Automobile Company had failed, Henry still had many friends and supporters with money. In late 1901 they put down the money to start the Henry Ford Company. But Henry and his investors had different ideas about what the company's goals should be. Just a few months later, Henry left the company to try to make it on his own.

Two failures would hurt the confidence of most people. But not Henry. In 1903 he got the chance to begin for a third time. The Ford Motor Company was formed with $28,000 that Henry had raised.

That summer the first Ford Motor Company car was built. It was called the Model A. This model had a bench seat for two people. The car became a big hit because it was strong and ran well. By late summer, people all over the country were ordering it.

▼ THE MODEL A with three people crowded into a car built for two

During its first fifteen months, Ford Motor Company built 1,708 cars. The company had grown from eleven to 125 employees. Designers worked with Henry to build new models—the Models B, C, F, and N.

Soon Henry was able to buy shares of the company owned by others, so that he owned most of the company himself. That meant he was in charge. He would stay in charge for the next forty years.

Ford made nine different models between 1903 and 1908, when the Model T was introduced. Henry was on his way to fame and fortune as his automobile caught on with Americans.

CHAPTER 5

A CAR FOR
EVERYONE

▲ ALL BUSINESS! Henry posed for this picture in his office as he was becoming successful.

"I will build a motorcar for the great multitude," Henry Ford once said. "It will be so low in price that no man making a good salary will be unable to own one." Henry and his team at the Ford Motor Company spent two years designing and planning that motorcar.

Henry wanted his new model to be bigger than any car he had produced. He also wanted it to be lighter. To do this, Henry used special lightweight steel called vanadium. The finished Model

T weighed about 1,200 pounds. It had room for five and ran on a powerful four-cylinder, twenty-horsepower engine. With its foot-controlled transmission, the two-speed car was also easy to drive.

A Bestseller and a New Home

The first Model T went on sale on October 1, 1908. It came in only one color: black. Black paint was chosen because it dried more quickly than paint of any other color. Customers loved the look and sturdy feel of the car. When the average cost of a car was $2,000 to $3,000, people loved the $825 price. Ads for the Model T proclaimed: "Even You Can Afford a Ford."

▼ FOR MANY AMERICANS, there was a Ford Model T in their future.

FORD MOTOR CARS

Illustrating Four Positions of the Model T Touring Car with Top

Serviceable and of very pleasing appearance from every view point

WATCH THE FORDS GO BY

◀ AN AD for the Model T shows it from three sides.

More than 10,000 Model Ts were sold in its first year. That was a record for any car. Ford advertised the Model T all across the country. Soon demand forced Henry to build a bigger and better factory at Highland Park, Michigan. Henry wanted the building to be full of natural light. The architect designed a special glass ceiling. It was so beautiful that the plant earned the nickname the Crystal Palace.

THE U.S. HIGHWAY SYSTEM

Today's modern highway system didn't always exist. In the early 1900s, "highways" followed the paths of pioneer wagon trails, such as the Santa Fe and Oregon Trails. Most of the roads were paved with concrete, though many were covered with cobblestone that caused bumpy travel.

As more and more people traveled by car, it became clear that better roads connecting cities had to be built. By 1925 there were more than 250 highways, but there was no plan to connect them or tie them together in any way. Each highway had a different name and different kinds of signs. Drivers were confused. People realized that there needed to be one system of interstate highways to make travel faster, more direct, and less confusing.

That didn't happen until 1954 when President Dwight Eisenhower signed a law to create an interstate highway system. Eisenhower wanted to

The Highland Park plant opened in 1910. Its main factory had four floors and was big enough for all work to be done under one roof.

Meanwhile, Henry continued to improve the way Model Ts were built. Better machines were always being developed. New ideas and experiments were always welcome in Henry's factory.

"Everything can always be done better than it is being done," Ford believed. The only thing Henry didn't make sure that good highways would connect U.S. cities from coast to coast to make it easier for troops to travel in times of war. This also made it easier for citizens to travel the country.

▲ THE INTERSTATE highway system began in the 1950s.

Today's interstate highways follow a pattern set up in the 1950s. There must be two lanes in each direction. Lanes must be twelve feet wide and there must be a ten-foot shoulder for cars to pull over if they are in trouble. Major highways that run north and south have an odd number. Highways going east and west have even numbers.

Thanks to Eisenhower, there are now more than 46,000 miles of interstate highways. United States highways are among the best in the world and help you get from one place to another as easily as possible.

consider changing was the color of the Model T. He joked that customers could have a Model T in any color "so long as it was black."

The Assembly Line

In 1913 Henry had one of his greatest ideas. It was based on something he and some of his workers had seen on a visit to a meatpacking plant in Chicago. There large pieces of meat that had to be cut into smaller pieces were carried along on an overhead trolley past a line of butchers. Each butcher removed a certain cut of meat until there was nothing left at the end of the line.

▼ CARS moved down an assembly line, making it easier and faster to build vehicles.

Henry wanted to try this idea in his factory. Each Ford worker would add a particular part to a Model T as the car was moved through the plant. It was called an assembly line, because a car was assembled as it moved down the line of workers.

▲ FORD dealerships, such as this one in Kansas, sprang up across America.

In 1914 the automatic conveyor belt at Highland Park could spit out a Model T every ninety-three minutes. The year before the assembly line was introduced, Ford produced 82,000 Model Ts. The next year, using the assembly line, production rose to 189,000 cars. By 1923, Ford's Highland Park assembly line produced two million Model Ts.

As more Model Ts were made, the price of the car dropped from $525 in 1912 to $345 in 1916. By 1912 there were seven thousand Ford dealers. As more Model Ts hit the road, Henry pushed for new and improved roads and more gas stations. The Model T was changing the way Americans lived. No longer was a car a luxury that only the rich could buy. Thanks to Henry Ford, more and more Americans owned cars and took vacations in them.

CHAPTER 6

A NEW
MIDDLE
CLASS

The assembly line meant that Model Ts could be built fast and at a low cost. But not everyone thought the assembly line was a good idea. Opponents worried that assembly line work made jobs boring. Doing the same tasks over and over required little thought and few skills.

On top of that, Ford workers earned just $2.38 for a nine-hour workday. Many were quitting their jobs. The company hired and trained new workers, but they didn't stay for very long. Henry had to do something about it.

▶ **HENRY FORD** became one of the most famous people in the United States.

On January 5, 1914, Henry shocked the world by announcing that he was going to raise the wage of Ford workers to five dollars a day. This was almost double what automobile workers at Ford and other car companies were earning! Henry also agreed to cut the workday by one hour to make it an eight-hour day. No business had ever offered double pay for less work.

▲ THOUSANDS OF WORKERS showed up at the Ford plant looking for $5-a-day jobs.

Ford's announcement made news all over the world. Many called Henry a hero of the working class. He was celebrated as a caring business leader.

To Henry, increasing the pay to five dollars a day was a smart business decision. Ford workers were happier and more productive. More Model Ts were being built and Ford was making more money. Between 1914 and 1916, the Ford Motor Company doubled its profits, from $30 million to $60 million. "The five dollar day was the greatest cost-cutting move I ever made," Henry said.

Better work output allowed Ford to lower the price of the Model T even more. Lower prices meant higher sales. Now even workers who built the Model T could afford to buy one. By offering higher pay and lower-priced cars, Henry helped to create a new middle class.

▲ FORD ADS were often designed to appeal to women.

Rich, Famous, and Still Down-to-Earth

Henry Ford's Model T, along with his unusual ideas about business, made him one of the wealthiest and most famous people in the United States—and the world. Magazines and newspapers wrote stories about him. Government leaders, including the president of the United States, wanted to know what he thought about the economy.

Henry Ford liked getting this kind of attention because it helped sell cars, but it didn't seem to change him from the farm boy from Dearborn he really was. He often said he didn't like "rich people."

Henry used his money and power to help others. He set up a program to help troubled young people. He hired people who had been jailed to work in his factory when no one else would give them a job. He set up a school to teach Ford workers from other countries how to speak English.

For all their wealth, Henry and Clara continued to live fairly simply. Henry didn't like fancy food or fancy clothes. Even though he could afford to buy all the new socks he could ever need, Clara continued to mend his old ones herself.

In 1912 Henry and Clara's son, Edsel, finished high school. Instead of going to college, Edsel decided to go to work for his father. He spent the next few years learning all aspects of the family business. The relationship between father and son was loving but difficult. Edsel's friends came from other wealthy Detroit families, and Henry often disapproved of them. Edsel married Eleanor Lowthian Clay, a member of a wealthy Detroit family, in 1916.

▼ THE FORD FAMILY in 1912

War and Politics

In 1914 World War I began in Europe. Henry was against the war and did not want the United States to get involved. Many people disagreed with Henry's views. They thought America should help bring about an end to the conflict. In late 1915 Henry chartered a ship to sail to Europe in support of peace. Henry's guests onboard

▲ **THE PEACE SHIP,** ready to set sail for Europe

were people who also hoped to end the conflict. The ship made headlines but failed to bring about peace.

▼ **A CAMPAIGN POSTER** from Henry's unsuccessful Senate race

HENRY FORD
For UNITED STATES SENATOR

PREPARED AND SUBMITTED BY
NON-PARTISAN FORD-FOR-SENATOR CLUB

This wasn't the last time Henry got involved in national and world affairs. In 1918 Henry ran for the U.S. Senate. Former President Theodore Roosevelt was one of Henry's biggest critics. He spoke out against Henry for his anti-war views. He also pointed out that Henry's only son, Edsel, did not fight in the war. It was a close race, but Henry lost.

Late in November 1918, Henry made a surprise announcement—he was stepping down as president of the Ford Motor Company. In 1919 Henry named his twenty-five-year-old son, Edsel, the new president of Ford. Edsel was hard-working, fair, and well-liked. But his relationship with his father continued to be difficult. The two men usually had different ideas about how to run the company. Sometimes Henry reversed decisions Edsel made. It soon became clear that even though Edsel had the title of president, Henry was still very much in charge.

ANOTHER SIDE OF
HENRY FORD

In 1918 Henry Ford bought a newspaper, the *Dearborn Independent*. Sadly, Henry used the newspaper to spread his hateful opinions about Jews. He said similar things in his books, including *My Life and Work*, published in 1923.

In 1927 Henry apologized for the terrible things he had written about Jews. Many people were still angry with Henry and believed he apologized because many Jews refused to buy Ford cars, so it was bad for his business. His image was forever harmed.

Years later, in 1938, Henry accepted an honor from Adolf Hitler, the German dictator who was determined to kill the Jewish people. By accepting the award—and by continuing to say nasty things about Jews in private—Henry seemed to prove that he still had bigoted ideas.

CHAPTER 7

AFTER THE
MODEL T

The Model T continued to be a huge hit not only in America but all over the world. In 1921 more than half of new cars bought were Model Ts. Over the years very little changed about the Model T, including its color—still always black.

In the mid 1920s, the Model T's price dropped to just $290. By then many customers were looking for more stylish cars. One competitor, Chevrolet, began to offer new models and choices and was taking away business from Ford.

◄ CHEVROLET had become a major competitor of Ford.

▲ HENRY AND EDSEL stand before their new Model A. The car came in several styles.

For a long time, Henry refused to make changes to the Model T, even though Edsel and others wanted him to. Sales of Chevrolets were rising, and sales of Model Ts were falling.

At last, on May 25, 1927, Henry announced that Ford would stop making the Model T. That day Henry said he was proud of the 15 million Model Ts that had been built. "It was the car that ran before there were good roads to run on," he said.

The Model A was the first new Ford model in nearly twenty years, and it was big news! Ford built the Model A at the company's new complex where the Detroit and Rouge Rivers meet. The complex was called the Rouge. It was called a complex because it wasn't just one factory. It was a collection of factories.

Henry wanted the Ford Motor Company to control everything needed to make cars. The complex could process coal from Ford-owned coal mines and also formed steel there. It had its own huge electric power plant, glass plant, cement plant, and a railroad with one hundred miles of track. Parts were made at the Rouge before they were assembled into cars.

When the Model A finally went on sale in December 1927, there were plenty of customers ready to buy it. They loved the look of it. The car came in four colors, which didn't include black!

What customers loved most about the Model A was the price—$385. That was less than the price of a Chevrolet. Ford's new car was a big hit.

▼ A WORKER in the well-lighted Rouge plant. Visitors came from all over to see it.

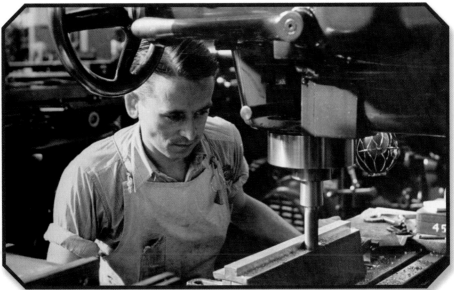

Ford had made a huge comeback with the Model A. More than four million were produced into 1931. By then sales at Ford and other auto companies had fallen. The country was facing hard economic times. Businesses were closing and millions of Americans had lost their jobs. This sad time in American history was called the Great Depression.

The Depression affected every business in America. In 1932 Ford had to cut workers' daily pay and let many go. Ford workers protested. Dearborn police clashed with the workers. The clash upset workers and the community. Ford was in trouble. What would Henry do next?

Henry Ford looked to the future when he designed cars, but he also cherished the past. Beginning in 1928, he built Greenfield Village next to the Henry Ford Museum in Dearborn, Michigan, to preserve that past. The village honors Henry's achievements as well as those of American inventors such as Thomas Edison, the Wright brothers, and George Washington Carver. Henry rebuilt and restored the homes, schools, and other buildings that he had lived and worked in. The village brings to life the sights and sounds of everyday life in America. Visitors experience more than three hundred years of history as they tour working farms, homes, main streets, and more. For more information, go to www.hfmgv.org.

CHAPTER 8

HENRY'S FINAL YEARS

During the early 1930s, Ford was producing cars in countries around the world. The Model Y was the first American car built for drivers outside the United States. It was sold in Europe in various versions for an incredible twenty-seven years! The Model Y helped Ford get through the toughest years of the Great Depression. In 1932 Ford introduced another new car in the United States. It was

◄ IN 1933 Henry was one of the richest people in the United States.

called the V-8 because it had a powerful eight-cylinder engine. Thanks to Edsel's ideas, the V-8 was considered one of the most stylish cars of the 1930s.

Unions Speak Out

Something else was happening in the 1930s. Automobile workers were organizing unions to protect the rights of workers. While other car companies worked with their unions, Henry refused. In 1937 men employed by Ford attacked and beat up some union organizers on the Rouge property. Photographs of the

▲ UNION MEMBERS and those against the unions fight in 1937.

beatings appeared in newspapers across the country. Henry's reputation was again tarnished.

In 1941 the union called for a strike at the Rouge. If the strike took place, production would come to a standstill. Finally, on June 20, 1941, Ford signed an agreement with the United Auto Workers union. In the end, workers at Ford received a much better deal than workers at any other American car company.

▲ THE JAPANESE ATTACK on Pearl Harbor, Hawaii, brought the U.S. into World War II.

Henry and the B-24

Meanwhile, European and Asian nations were fighting in World War II. Once again Henry spoke against the war. He wanted America to stay out. That was not to be. On December 7, 1941, Japan attacked the United States naval base at Pearl Harbor, Hawaii. Congress responded by declaring war on Japan.

America's attention was entirely on the war. In 1942, Ford had just one customer: the United States government. Ford built an airplane factory in Willow Run, Michigan. It was the largest factory of its kind in the world. At Willow Run, workers built B-24 Liberty Bomber planes. By August 1944, Willow Run was producing one B-24 each day!

While the nation was focused on war, Edsel Ford was fighting a terrible battle of his own. On May 26, 1943, when he was just forty-nine years old, Edsel died from cancer. The Ford family was grief-stricken, and so were Ford workers, who mourned their leader. Henry named himself the new president of Ford. But things were different this time. Henry was nearly eighty and his health was failing. He couldn't do the job for long.

In September 1945, Edsel's son, Henry Ford II, was named

▶ HENRY never wanted the U.S. to go to war.

In 1936 Edsel Ford and two Ford Motor Company leaders set up the nonprofit Ford Foundation. Henry left most of his $500 million fortune to the foundation when he died. Today the foundation's goals are to strengthen democracy, reduce poverty, promote international cooperation, and advance human achievement. The foundation operates separately from the Ford Motor Company.

In 1969 the foundation gave one million dollars to Children's Television Workshop to create a new show called *Sesame Street*. Since then the foundation has continued to support public television and the arts. It has also given money to help reduce poverty and the spread of AIDS.

MYSTERY PERSON

the new president of Ford. He was just twenty-eight. Henry Ford II helped bring the company into the modern era. He also worked hard to rescue his grandfather's reputation.

Farewell, Henry

On April 7, 1947, at the age of eighty-three, Henry Ford died at his Michigan home on the banks of the Rouge River. Clara was by his side. People all over the world mourned his death. World leaders and ordinary citizens sent tribute messages to the Ford home.

More than 100,000 mourners paid their last respects to Henry at Greenfield Village before his funeral at a church in Detroit. After the service he was buried in a nearby cemetery. In Detroit, flags hung at half-mast. Other American car companies stopped work at their factories for a moment of silence.

All over the world, people remembered the man who built the first affordable car for the masses. They also remembered Henry as the man who helped create a middle class in America by raising worker pay while lowering the price of his cars.

Henry forever changed the way cars were built. He could be difficult and stubborn, but more than anything else, Henry Ford will always be remembered as the man who put the world on wheels—helping people leave the horse and carriage behind.

▼ CITIZENS patiently line up to say good-bye to Henry Ford in April 1947.

TALKING ABOUT
HENRY

▲ John Metz

TIME For Kids spoke with John Metz, a curator with The Henry Ford, about Henry's life and his ideas. The Henry Ford includes Greenfield Village, an IMAX theater, and several attractions.

Q: *Why did Henry start up Greenfield Village?*

A: In early 1925 Henry announced his plans to build Greenfield Village, a museum and historical village to house his growing collection of Americana—items showing the culture, way of life, and history of the United States.

Q: *How is Henry's concern for education shown in your exhibits?*

A: At Greenfield Village guests can visit one-room

▲ THE WHITE HOUSE in the photo was once the home of the Wright brothers. It was moved to Greenfield Village from Dayton, Ohio.

schoolhouses and the home where Noah Webster wrote his famous dictionary in 1828. Henry had also started a school where students learned by doing. Today there is a high school with four hundred students.

Q: *If Henry Ford were alive today, what do you think he would be doing to help protect or improve the environment?*

A: We think Henry believed in achieving a balance between nature and technology. We know that he loved nature—he enjoyed camping and he loved birds. He used water-powered machines to make electricity at his home. This suggests that he believed in the need for natural, nonpolluting power sources. We can also guess that Henry believed in sustainability through his work in coming up with ways to use soybeans and other crops in industry.

▶ TAKE A RIDE in a Model T at Greenfield Village. The car celebrated its one hundredth birthday in 2008.

HENRY FORD'S
KEY DATES

1863 Born near Dearborn, Michigan, on July 30

1865 The U.S. Civil War ends.

1888 Marries Clara Bryant and moves to a farm in what is now Dearborn, Michigan

1893 Henry and Clara's only child, Edsel, is born

1896 Henry builds his first automobile, called the Quadricycle, and drives it through the streets of Detroit

1912 New Mexico and Arizona become the forty-seventh and forty-eighth states.

1903 Forms Ford Motor Company

1908 Introduces the Model T, an affordable instant hit

1913-14 Introduces the assembly line and five dollars daily pay at his plant

1918 Loses a close race for a U.S. Senate seat in Michigan

1940 The automatic dishwasher is invented.

1947 Dies April 7, in Michigan